Write From
The Heart 2

Write From The Heart 2

ERICA HICKS JENKINS

ARPress
ILLUMINATING IDEAS
EMPOWERING VOICES

ARPress
45 Dan Road Suite 5
Canton MA 02021

Hotline: 1(888) 821-0229
Fax: 1(508) 545-7580

Ordering Information:
Quantity sales. Special discounts are available on quantity purchases by corporations,associations, and others. For details, contact the publisher at the address above.

Printed in the United States of America.

ISBN-13:   Softcover   979-8-89356-430-3
              eBook   979-8-89356-429-7

Library of Congress Control Number: 2024904691

CONTENTS

WRITE FROM THE HEART

The words just flow from the tip of my pen
Telling tales of where I might go or
Where I have been

Who says it has to be true, you really could not tell
If it were true or not
They are my thoughts, my feelings;
It flows from my heart

Life's experience is a good topic, the disappointments
Would be a good one too
That is what I write about so believe that most
Of my words are true

Even if I have not experienced it someone I know
May have and passed it on to me
So in many ways I have written things that can
Happen to anyone can't you see

It is real life's good, bad, and evil from the middle,
End or from the start
Not only do I write the truth, I write from the heart

TOTAL RESTORATION

Growing up in the church was a big part of
Being raised in the south
Having good manners was taught well
I was told when to open and close my mouth

I do have my own personal relationship with god
And it is a plus
For prayer and faith in god from day to day is a must

Sometimes I lose focus and often times get sidetracked
From the wares of life and that I hate
But god will always guide me and set my crooked
Paths once again straight

For god did not say we would not have trials
And tough times to get through
What he said was when your load get too heavy, it
Is then that he would carry you

He has never failed me although I have
Often times failed myself
At times I have felt so low that I
Thought even god could not help

2

It is then that I went back to my roots to
What I have heard over and over again
Trust Jesus you will find he is always
Your friend

When life deals you a bad hand know that god
Is there and will never leave you
He will provide you with all you need to get
You through
God has made me stronger than I thought I
Would ever be
He will do it for you to open your heart
And eyes so you can be free

My god is good at all times and that is not an exaggeration
He touched my mind, body, soul and spirit and I am so
Grateful for my total restoration

ALL I NEED

When we first met, I thought it would just be
A fling or two
Look how far we have come- how much
We have been through

Our friendship – boy did it grow
How much more will it grow, we do not know

For now, let's just take it one day at a time
Afterall, things do get better with time

Believe it or not for it is so true
I am so thankful just for you

Words cannot express the joy you bring
You are just what the doctor ordered –
My sweet thing

I am solely yours even if you are not quite
Mine
Of course you are mine when we are together
And that is just fine

You know just the right thing to say and
Always the right thing to do
That is why I can honestly say – today,
Tomorrow, forever – all I need
Is you!!!!

HOPE

I hope tomorrow comes
That you may finish what
You started yesterday…

I hope tomorrow comes
So that you may correct
The mistakes you made
Yesterday…..

I hope tomorrow comes
That you may experience
Something new…..

But do not put off what
Can be done today for
Tomorrow because tomorrow
Is not promised to any
Of us……

May all your work be done
Today in preparation
Of a better tomorrow

May all your days (including tomorrow)
Be filled
With the grace of god and
Much success…

PEACE IN YOUR NEW FOUND DWELLING

As sad as I am to see you go
I am gonna miss you a lot –that
You already know

Not seeing your smiling face or getting
My good morning cheer
Will make me sad when I approach the
Gate and you are not there

But i am happy for you nevertheless
As a gate keeper you are the best

Please keep in touch by phone or letter
I am not asking you to promise, but
By god you better!!

My friend, take care of yourself and rhett
Your fearless, wee hour wee weeing pet

I bid you later not farewell or goodbye
You will never really be rid of me my friend
So don't even try

I am not gonna cry, scream and ok
No yelling
I am gonna miss you but I wish you
Much love, happiness and peace in
Your newfound dwelling....

THANK YOU

It is wonderful people like you
That make unbearable things in
Life bearable. You were there for
Us… you called, stopped by,
Prayed, hugged and showed untiring
Caring love in so many ways -
Thank you…may god bless and enrich
Your lives in a very special way!!!

We know that "thank you" is such a small
Way to compliment the unselfish and big
Hearted way you have blessed our
Family during such a difficult time. But
We are thankful from the bottom of our
Hearts….

DIAMOND DUST AFFAIR

Who was I kidding this relationship
is actually make believe
All we are really out to do is lie, cheat and
deceive

What you do not know will not hurt or
So I was told
But I also know what happens in the dark
Come to the light, all your skeltons
In your closet exposed

I am living in a fantasy I need to wake up
Before it is too late
I thought I was blessed to meet you – i even
Called it fate

Of course wrong is always wrong and
It cannot ever be right
But even in a losing battle no one
Wants to lose the fight

Watching where we go – trying our
Best to be discreet
If you put your business out there, it will
Surely hit the streets

Sure you are good to me better
Than anyone has ever been
I even called you Mr. Wonderful – my
Closest and dearest friend

You belong to someone else who has papers on you
For you vowed your love to them and promised
To be true

Vows are so sacred and should not be broken
And that is the truth
I know that it was wrong, no excuses what
The use

At first it did not matter I really did
Not care,
But now it is time to stop this mess and
Put an end to this diamond dust affair

WE WILL CHERISH YOUR LIFE

We can hardly believe that it has been a
Year ago since you left us here
We miss you so much but we have loving memories
That we will always share

You were the chain in the family that kept us
All together 0 very close
Your loving nurturing nature is what
We will miss most

You laid the foundation that will forever,
make the family bond strong
Thank you for all you did for us and
The life lesson that will remain with us
A lifetime long

We will miss you dearly mom just sleep on
and take your rest we loved you but god always
love you best

Heaven has gained a new angel up above
A dear angel with undying love

You were one of a kind – a loving mother, grandmother,
Sister, aunt, neighbor, friend and wife
we thanked the lord for you and each new day we
Will find ways to cherish your life

WALKING BY FAITH

Faith is the substance of things hoped for and the evidence of
things not yet seen.
It actually mean to claim things not yet
Materialized -- like claiming victory over your dreams

When you can do this you put the holy spirit
In charge completely
The holy spirit takes over and you will feel
Its strength so deeply

There is nothing better than relieving
Yourself of burdens and just letting go
It frees your mind, body, soul and make your
Spirit soar to high from low

You can wake up in the morning excited to face the day
You can lay down at night and sleep soundly
After you pray

Of course all your troubles are not over
But your load is much easier to bear
To live with the spirit alive is to live free from fear

When nothing can take your joy or break into your mist
It is like ruling your own state of mind with
The holy spirit being your iron fist

It is like telling your mountain to get out of
Your way, just like the savior saith
When you experience the true holy spirit
It is then that you are
Walking by faith

SAY A PRAYER

Prayer always changes things and what a joy prayer brings no
matter how much prayer you get there is always a need for more –
for no amount of prayer is too much
So in essence prayer is just the right touch

So take time to say a prayer for someone else even
Before praying for yourself
Then pray for your needs __ it is like self help

Take time to pray for a neighbor or a peer
For it is the unselfish prayer god likes to hear

Pray much for your enemies because god loves them too
Praying for them may help, not harm you

Pray for your coworkers, family members and friends
For they may be going through
Pray that they realize that they are being thought of
And prayed for too

Say a prayer for the homeless, sick and shut in, the less
Fortunate for they count as well
Pray for the above average, they may be in trouble
And do not show it so we cannot tell

Take time to pray for the mentally challenged or
The unstable
[pray a thanks for the roof over your head, clothes on your back
and food on your table

Pray for being blessed to see this day for tomorrow
For you may never come
Take3 time to pray for peace to overshadow confusion
At least some

Pray for patience, guidance, understanding and
Wisdom for sure
Pray that your mind is clear and your heart to be pure

Take time to pray for your government, president,
Congress, senate and your own mayor
Do not ever miss an opportunity and never end
Or start any day before you say a prayer

SOMEONE TO LOVE ME

I am looking for a man that is tall, dark, handsome
And fancy free
I am looking for someone – someone to love me

He need not be rich or famous,)) just hones and willing to work
For i am tired of the old lazy, old broke man that act like a jerk

If you are mature and have a since of humor; of course
That will be a plus
But having a car and a j-o-b is a must

You need not approach me as prince charming on a white horse
Just be yourself and act like a true man, of course

You do not need to be with me 24-hours a day or seven days a
week
Please be strong, loving gentle and meek

Treat me like the lady that I am and give me plenty of respect
That is not just what I want, that is what i expect

I do not ask for much I just want to be loved right
I want to be cuddled in your arms like I should at night

I want to be able to look in your eyes and know it is truth I see
And feel sure that you are that special someone—someone
To love me

Not only do I want to hear you say it, I want to feel it too
I want to believe that; your love is really true

I have been hurt so much: used and abused
Now I want real love and everything else I will refuse

I deserved to be cared for because I have paid the price
For i have given so much of myself only to be taken
Advantage of because I was nice

You are looking for me and I am looking for you
You are a true, loving individual; of which
There are only a few

Where are you, oh where can you be?
You are that special someone – someone
To love me

DON'T DOUBT ME

When I said I loved you, I meant it
When I feel this way what else can it be
So whenever you get discouraged,
Don't doubt me

The tings I do and have done for you, I did
Because I love you
You are in my heart, my sour, you are my life
Don't you see
Whenever something goes wrong try to fix it, but
Don't doubt me

Whenever we are apart, I long to be near you as I can
Your longing for me Me loving you, you loving me,
That is the way it should be

As your questions, speak your piece, bring out things
We need to discuss but never – because as long as we are
Together there is no need –so don't doubt me

WITHOUT YOU

I sit her alone wondering what to do
I realize I would not have this problem if and
Only if I were with you

I miss you so much that it hurts to think of just how much
I miss everything – your kiss, your smile,
Your touch

If guess you already figured that I am lost without you
I do not know what today or what to do

Without you there is a part of me that is missing
I cannot quite put my finger on it but I know
It is not there
I could figure it out if you were not very far,
but very near

Of course you know it, I feel it, and it is true
I would be totally lost without you

GOD'S GRACE

By the grace of God I woke up this morning
Able to start my day
Confident that god would help me in all situations
Anyhow any way

Thankful for all the things I have been blessed to possess
I stood up and stretched and thought I would get dressed

As I picked up a garment something made me realize
That starting this day or any day without prayer
Would not be very wise

Di stepped back into my room from the hallway
Kneeled down in front of my bead head hung, hands
Folded in preparation to pray

As my mouth the words just tumbled out
I was surprised, for I never knew I had so much
To pray about

Realizing that no matter what I want, God always
Supply me with all I need
All I have to do is step back, put god first in my life
And follow his lead

As I ended my prayer, my body felt warmer for the
Sun was shining on my face
For I did my duty and will always thank my creator for
I know
I cannot make it without God's grace

A DADDY NOT A FATHER

I wanted a family, and you did too
At least that is what you said,
But it was not true

You left me without saying goodbye –mu heart all torn
You left me before our child was even born

You walked out without an explanation
How could you walk away from your obligation?

It took both of us to create this life
Now it is my child that will have to suffer – not me; the ex-wife

Anyone can father a child but it takes a special man
To be a dad
It is a special bond between a father and a child --
No matter if it is a girl or a lad

One day you may need this same child to help you in some way
I hope I am around to see the look on your face when our
Child will treat you the same way

I am not asking you for a favor to do something for us
Now, so don't even bother
Afterall, right now my child need a daddy not a father

YOU DESERVE BETTER

Settling for less than you deserve is not planned it is something that
happens – you have no control over it
Knowing that something is not working but not wiling
To give in or quit

Only serving what you want to see even though the true
Picture is right in front of your eyes
Getting used and abused – never getting the truth but
Always getting lies

You are not the first and you will not be the last
Do not change because of others failures be true to
Yourself and hold fast

You gave of yourself so earnestly and with good intent
Be not be afraid to admit or talk about it – use
Family and friends to vent

Show your emotions it is natural and something we must all do
So cry, scream, get angry then sad, it will help you get through

You were taken advantage of, it was because you are a good
Person – pure at heart
Think of this as not the end, but as a fresh start

Sometimes you have to lose in order to gain
Do not let this hinder you for you will sustain

Afterall you are a strong person, a fighter, a winner
A go=getter
This is not a setback it is a step up where you need to be
And besides you deserve better

GOD WILL GUIDE YOU

Things may not go as you wish they will
When there is a void in your heart that nothing
Seem to fill

Do not give up or despair
For god is real and is always very near

You may not see him or hear his call
But he loves us one and all

There is no big "I" or little "u"
God will help us all through

Change may not come in this form or another
Change will come for all of us,
Yes my sister and my brother

When all else fails give god a try
You heard those words all your life
Now it is time to find out why

There may a bend in the road that
You cannot see around

Cast your burdens on god the true friend
You have found

He may not come when you want him but he will
Always bring you through
For why me you are at your lowest point
And see no way out, that is when
God will guide you

SPERM DONOR

We have been together for over three years
You were so sweet at first, so sincere

I thought that you were the best thing since apple pie
Now I look at our situation and wonder why

To hear of my conception should have been good news
But all you have done since is sing the blues

Maybe you are afraid of the new responsibility to be
Instead of just the two of us, it will be harder with three

To make matters worst you even picked up a new friend
Yeah a female, and you lied to the end

You have not done a thing since your son was conceived
All you do now is lie, at first your lies id did believe

Every chance you got before you warmed my bed
I guess at the time it was just a nice place to
Lay your head

Maybe you intend for this to be temporary, not
Long lasting
But I will continue to stay on bend knees and
Keep fasting

Why am I surprised all the signs were there
That shows how much in love I was in, just wanted you near

I guess the old saying is true – your testicles were just
A loaner
Because thus far all you have been a sperm donor

FILLS THE VOID IN OUR HEARTS

As mile that can warm the coldest heart and put a
Smile on any face
Very soft spoken and filled with such grace

Like a ray of sunshine that used to greet us and the kind
Words once said
Si just some of the good impressions on us that
Knowing you has made

Gone are your sweet smiles that put laughter in our hearts
The same smiles that will keep you with us event though
We are apart

You always knew how to bring joy at all times; night or day
Those are things that will forever be embedded in our
Memories I will say

We know that you are really gone, you are just away
We know we will meet again some place, some day

As long as we remember you, you will not really be gone
For fond memories of you will help you forever live on

You were always a kind heart, a devoted friend and a
Loving mother
Always doing what you had to do to bring joy to another

Sleep on our cherished loved one and take your rest
We can feel comfort in knowing we loved you but
God loved you best

Many days, months, even years may pass while we are apart
But loving, kind, fond memories and the goodness of god will
Help fill the void in our hearts

DREAM LOVER

When I close my eyes I feel so secure
You will join me at that moment I am always sure

We unite and become one when we are together
May this feeling last forever

You are all I ever wanted and dreamed that you would be
Finally, I feel that someone is sincerely loving me

I can be myself with you for there is no need to hide
For you know everything I am feeling inside

You make me feel like no one has before
My self-esteem and confidence has been restored

I can do anything I want to do
As long as I am with you

The precious hours we spend together are so special to me
For when I open my eyes who knows where you might be

If not you, there would be no other
Because you are all I need – my dream lover

Night skies brings us together as daylight often keeps us apart
But all through the day I carry you around in my heart

When my eyes close it is only you I long to see
May think I am fantasizing but you are my reality

As dawn nears i grab your hands and hold really tight
For I know our meetings are and can only be at night

Sweet dreams I have all night through
Feeling so alive and free being with you

You are a blessing that I did discover
I live for my nights for that is when we can be together
Yes me and you – dream lover

DON'T LET GO

Did you ever dream of dong or being something and
Backed down out of fear
To attain your goal you have to believe in yourself
And you will get there

Did you listen to a parent, a co-worker, or a peer?
They were being concerned because they care

Failure is always a hard lesson to learn
Success is the key here and can be easily earned

Youi have to trust and believe in yourself and keep
Your eyes open for an open door
Soak your feet then they are in pain – rub your
Shoulders when they are sore

Give it all you have and watch your success grow
Hold fast to your dreams and don't let go

First there is one thing you must do
Believe in yourself do not wait
For others to believe in you

Life if full of risks and chances to take
Life is full of decisions always to make

Taking chances is a must and that is a fact
You can do anything you want to just
Keep your dreams intact

Believe in yourself and let you light shine
That will always s give you a peace of mind

Put god first in all you want to do
Watch how god can win the battle for you

Relax, believe and take it slow
Hold fast to your dreams and don't let go

If Michael Jordan would have listed to what others
He would not have been a basketball star
I challenge you to believe in yourself and
Accept who you are

If at first you do not succeed try and try again
The only failure is giving up my friend

Education is vital so find out all you need to know
Hold fast to your dreams and don't let go

CRIES FALLING ON DEAF EARS

A newborn baby born to a drug addicted mother
The homeless living inside of cardboard boxes or
Under bridges for cover

A battered wife, a shattered life are included in this fight
Trying to be heard or helped with all their might

The unemployed standing in line only to be turned around
The elderly that should receive welfare are the ones
That are turned down

Abused and neglected kids or kids that just run wild
Do anyone care what happens to the future of
A young child?

The disease inflicted are not left out, they are on
This road too
These are people who need help just like me
And just like you

For the many years you have been on a job and
To this day make the same pay
Believe the words of dr. King for you shall
Overcome one day

For the many of you living in a home with no heat,
Water or even a rug on the floor
You have no air when it is hot, just lucky enough
To have a front door

We are all in this together whether you are right,
Average or poor
No matter how much you have or how much you lack
You can always use more

For the handicapped, the disabled, the mentally ill,
The slow learning too
There has got to be a way out, something someone
Can do

It is really a shame that through all the years
And through all the hard shed tears
Most of those cries and more too are still
Just cries falling on deaf ears

PARENTS

God's gift to children to love, to guide to protect
To teach how to be well mannered and to respect

To take me under their wing and mold me in the way
They want me to grow
To tell me that it always right to do right and when
I am wrong to tell me so

To help me understand the importance of faith
And to know the power of god's grace

To lend an ear when I need to talk
To cuddle me when I cry, to help me pick
The right path to walk

Oh how lost a child would be without their parents, some
Are so blessed they do not know how much
Not until their parents are gone or are out of touch

I am blessed and I know I am to be a product of parents
I can be honored to claim
If you have parents, you should tell them you
Love them now and hug them too; I love my parents
And I am going to do the same…

LOVE ME IN YOUR HEART

Let/s be friends first then lovers, i believe the saying goes
Where we will end up nobody knows

Let's take it slow, one day at a time
Let's not lose ourselves at the drop of a dime

You make me feel special, yes you do
I think I make you feel the same way too

Things are getting heated I can feel it in my heart
But let's not rush things, that may make us grow apart

Let's take the time to get to know each other first
We must not let it be a quencher for our sexual thirst

I love the way you make me feel when I am with you
It is the way you look at me and the loving things you do

I know you are eager to hold me in your arms
But I cannot allow myself to succumb to your loving charm

I want you to respect me so do not be alarmed
You must first love me in your heart before
You love me in your arms

Trust me my love and you will see
Patience is a virtue, that should be practiced by you and me

Do not blame for putting you through this test
If you cannot pass this part you can forget
About the rest
As our friendship grows stronger as each day pass
I want to do all I can to make sure we last

I love the way I bring a smile to your face
I love the closeness and the tenderness of
Your loving sweet embrace

Just let things happen naturally and give
Our relationship a fresh start
And you will be able to truly love me, but you will
First love me in your heart

ONCE IN A LIFETIME LOVE

Words cannot express the things I am about to say
One could only imagine what makes me feel this way

It only comes once in a lifetime and sometimes it does
Not last long
No matter if it is not by choice or if you are right or wrong

It happens so fast you cannot see it coming or feel it turn on
So enjoy it while you can before it is gone

When you came into my life I was a hopeless case
But you brought joy into my life and a smile on my face

I knew it was love right from the start
The way you made me feel and took control of my heart

I know that no one can ever replace you or do the things you do
For you are one of a kind and you are good at that too

When we reached our peek trouble started to arise
Even now when I think of that pain it bring tears
to my eyes

Thoughts of you make me happy sometimes sad
That is when I remember times shared and all the fun we had

But let this be only a lesson even if you never become
Or I your wife
Never fail to let someone who cares come in and enrich
Your life

It is very strong and can be compared only to heaven up above
So be thankful and feel fortunate if you ever get a chance
To experience the "once in a lifetime love"

I AM HERE TO STAY

When we met I had no idea I would feel this way
You and I be if you jump try a blessing what else
Can I say

I know you have been hurt, I have been hurt too
So do not think that I do not have doubts just like you do

Trust is the key here and it must exist
Trust me, I will trust you for my heart cannot resist

Always be honest, loyal and true
And in return, my love, I will do the same for you

When something goes wrong do not talk to your friend
Trust me enough and on my loyalty depend

I hope you can see what your doubts have done to me
It has hurt me deeply and I am as frail as can be

I want to do all I can to make sure we last
But you cannot live in the present or future if
You are still living in your past

Do not base our relationship on what you have
Been through years ago
Just take one step at a time, be patient and
Let our love grow

Let me love you as I want, in my own way
For if you do so earnestly I am here to stay

AN INTERNET AFFAIR

I never thought I would live to see the day
That a computer would aid the deceitful this way

You told lies to your buddies in the chat room
They believed what you said was true
Or so they assumed

You betrayed me and yourself for that matter
All my hopes and dreams you did shatter

What happened to growing old together as you said?
Now you cannot even look me in the eyes, what a
Mess you have made

I dare you say it was a man thing I would not understand
For what you did and how you did it you are less than
And not worthy of calling yourself a man

You are a coward, a thief, a jack of all trades
You hid behind lies, stole my heart and my soul,
I am afraid

One day you will regret how you tore our union apart
If you did not want me, you should have said so
From the start

Not to mention how you stole from our housetop
Take care of another
And had the nerve to act like you were all that,
Oh brother

Could not even pay the bills let alone keep a
Roof over our head
Fooling without I could have gone insane or could be dead

You were not worth all the pain and headaches I went through
Someday someone may do the same things to you

Mine how you treat someone is what you always teach
It is a shame that you did not practice what you preached

You were not sorry for hurting me, you never apologized
Or shed one tear
I hope you will never have to feel the pain I have felt all for
The sake of a few thrills in an internet affair

ALWAYS IN YOUR HEART

You have lost someone very dear to you
You are not alone for I have too

You may miss them very much, much, even their smile
Well sit back and listen to me for a while

You cannot hear their voice, but though you are apart
They will forever live on in your heart

When you are feeling low and think you are alone
Remember you will have to travel the same path
Your loved one has gone

I know you loved them, but god loved them best
It is just life's way of putting us to a test

We all must pass this way but once and at our own pace
Just love one another while you are on this race

Think of past times you have shared with those
That are gone
And always remember you are never alone

You cannot see them, feel their touch, or hear their
Voices but that does not mean that they are not
There thought we are apart
Just keep the alive by forever carrying them as close
As you can always in our heart

UNDYING LOVE

True love is hard to find
But we found it my love
Our union is unique, and it is blessed by god above

Time has come and gone so fast
But our undying love will forever last

Who would have thought we would still be?
Together today
May God bless us with many more years i pray

To our union we were blessed with a son
And together baby me and you – are one

In this game of love together we will
Always win
We have lasted ten years—I can
Hardly wait to experience the next ten

Happy anniversary today and always too
Every day I enjoy celebrating me and you

If I live one hundred years, there will never
Be another
To take your loving place in my heart,
My best friend and lover

So let us continue to enjoy each other as
God has planned because we fit together
Like a glove
I will forever love you with all my heart
And know that you will always have
My undying love

SIGNS OF A CHEATEN' MAN

He came home with lipstick on his collar
Just got paid wallet empty not even a dollar
Leaving home early, getting home late
You are a married man, you shouldn't date

Phone rings, I answer, caller hangs up on me
Phone rings again, you answer, caller speaks what else can it be
We live in the same house but rarely see each other
You must be giving my love to another

We sleep in the same bed but barely touch
What happened to the sweet kisses I miss so much
You used to kiss me when you return home
And also when you depart

If you did not plan to continue this, why did you ever start?
If you want someone else, why are you still with me
If you tell the truth I would gladly set, you free
What happened to the love notes you used to leave everywhere?
Now you barely look at me or show you even care

The way we are living is not the right way
I wish I could leave but all I do is stay

You let our bills all get past due
I can't believe I thought I knew you

Not that I was being nosey, but I noticed condoms in your car
I guess now I know what your late meetings are
I asked you, and you accused me of having an affair
You played hurt and disappointed and acted as if you cared

That didn't last long the pattern is still the same.
But one day my love, your unfaithfulness will bring you shame
As I was doing the laundry, out of your pocket fell a love note Signed
you know who
I wish there was a name, then I would know who too

I have been good to you and really deserve more
I have taken all I can take my next step is out the door
When you come home and find your family all packed up and gone
You will feel as I feel now and that is so alone

So a message to all women, young and old alike
Before you say I do, please make sure your man is right
If he mistreat you just leave don't give him another chance
For that will be the beginning of the end of your romance

I live one hundred years I will never understand
But please take heed and learn these signs
They are signs of a cheating man!!

ON YOUR OWN

To leave a comfortable nest to build your own
You may find that you will feel very alone
Be strong, be brave and always stand tall
For there is always someone wishing you will fall

The first step is always the hardest one to take
But that is one step you must not hesitate to make
People you look up to may not help you
Or may try to change your mind
Taking advice from someone you really trust may be
Like the blind leading the blind

Not that you should turn deaf ears on all the advice you get
But use it for what it is and don't be afraid to get your feet wet
It is now or never if you want to be on your own
Not just to prove a point or just show you are grown

Do it because it is what you want to do
The experience will be a benefit to you
Don't turn your back on your friends and loved ones
That wouldn't be fair
For if you fall or need a shoulder maybe they will be there

But don't be afraid to take a chance for that is what life is full of
Make your own decisions and trust in the God above
But respect the ones that truly care and love you best
For they are trying to prepare you for life's greatest test

Independence is one thing that we may all want one day remember,
You can believe most of what you see
And only half of one do or say

So do it for independence, for self-satisfaction,
Not to prove you are grown
Just be careful, keep faith and let your friends and loved ones
Help you especially when you are on your own

THE WORLD'S MOST PRECIOUS MOTHER

I looked in all the stores and at a sales ad
But of the things I wanted for you were things you had
A dress would have been nice, a pair of shoes would do
But for this special day I wanted something for you

Jewelry always makes a good gift, so that is where I took a look
Sorry mom the prices there were a bit too much for my pocketbook
Not to say you are not worth all the jewelry in all the stores, in all The
states, I just did not have the money it takes

I knew you would love me no matter what I had to give. For after
All I am, and always will be your kid.
I did not give up because I could not afford that,
I looked some more to see \where to get my #1 person's gift at

I looked high, I look low
I looked so hard I did not know where else to go
Then it hit me and hit me hard.
I could go buy you a very special card

So to hallmark I went in a flash
For I knew my purchase would not take a lot of cash
I picked up a card to read and the words said,
"Mother without you there would be no me"
And those few words made me see

It is not about buying gifts and spending all you possess
It is really about showing your love and appreciation
For a special mother and mom you are the best

Not just today, tomorrow and always too,
There will never be another as special to me as you
I decided to do what I do best and that is to express myself in Words
for they are words that should be seen as well as heard

I know you feel it and know it anyway, so not only because it is
Mother's day but today and everyday, I am glad that you are you I
Love you mother today, tomorrow and always too

You are an inspiration, a gift, an idol; you are all that and more
Because your heart is where caring and pure love always pour
You are a special blessing, a portrait of love sent here for us like And
angel from god above.

I am thankful for all that I have, for not only do I have more than
One sister and more than one brother I have what so few can say
They have I have you, and you are the greatest and the world's Most
precious mother!!!!!!!!!!!

A SEXUALLY ABUSED CHILD

You took away my innocence without a thought did you ever stop
To think about the emptiness your act has brought

Gone is my virginity before I knew what it was or understood it
I wonder why or what was the cause I cannot find an answer that
Seems to fit

I have no happiness, and my self-esteem is shot
All others my age re talking about crushes they've got
When I was younger, I thought it was my fault that this happened
To me but time has healed me some and now I see

You are at fault and someday you will pay you will feel the same
Pain I feel or something similar someday
Maybe you are sick, you can get help I hope you are a coward
That is what you are a dope

I cannot share my secrets of my first time for love with my friends
they do not know the heartache thoughts of my first time brings
I hope you lay awake like I have and sometimes still do yes I have
Cried myself to sleep many nights because of you

Prayer changes things that is what my mother always say
So, when things were rough,
All I had to do was kneel down and pray

There is a part of me that you killed and put to shame
But I cannot give up and just let you win
I know sometimes things get rough but I will try again

May God bless you and have mercy on your soul
Yes the same God that has healed me and once again
Make me fell whole

I have learned to forgive you but
I will never forget what you did to me
I will remember the ugly acts, but prayer has set me free

I pray that not another child goes through what
I did it is no piece of cake it is a big burden for a kid
As with anything time is a healer and time will heal the pain
Self-love and self-respect will be what is gained

Remember through ever cloudy day there is a silver lining
The cloud will not be over you always sometime
Your sun will be shining

A SPECIAL FRIEND

Big hearted and gentle as can be
A loving friend always to me
Respects me and of that I am proud

Rowdy at time but never gets too loud
Young at heart and always willing but
Never follow the crowd

Gracious as a lion and sneaky too
Righteous as can be, that is why I am
Glad you are you
Approaches everything with a positive attitude
Very arrogant and blunt but you are never rude

Easy going, sweet, a gentleman in every way
Sincere with everything you do and all that you say
That is why you are special today and all days

You have stuck with me through thick and through thin
And I thank god for you over and over again
Gurl you my precious, very special friend…

WHAT IS AN OLDER SISTER?

A special friend
A gentle touch
One who cares for you so much

One who tires so hard to save you from pain
By giving and teaching from the experience
She had gained

One who shares her inner-most thoughts
And shares a little of heat she was taught

One who shares the woes and whims of men
Who have you prepared before you begin?

Sure, sometimes she is hard and seems mean too
She is just trying to make sure you what you
Should do

She knows better, she is older and wiser than
You and your peers
So do the old gal a favor, let her save you
Some tears

Thank god if you have sisters, especially and older one
And if you are really blessed to have even more, then
You, like me, should have lots of fun

Sure, they get on your nerves and make you mad as can be
Take heed and listen it will pay, you will see

I thank God for my oldest sisters, and am very grateful
For the eldest one of all
She is the one with the most guts
And whim even if she is not tall

We have argued, we have made each other mad,
We have done all that all other sisters do

That is why I am thankful to god for an older sister,
And I am glad that sister is you!!!!!!!!!!!!!!!!!!!!!!!!!!!!!!!!!!!!!!!

A MOTHER

Not just a pretty face
She is the ruler and keeper of the human race
She is always there in your time of need
And yes, this woman is a friend indeed

She has eased your pain and dried your tears
And carried for you for many, many years
It matters not if she gave birth or not
This is a lady you will feel lucky you've got

For giving birth alone doesn't make you a mother
It takes kind loving hearts that can care and protect another
If you have ever cared for a youngster, took them under your wing
And taught them what to and not to do
In a sense you are a mother,
For that is what makes you a mother too

If you ever sat up all night to ease the pain and sullen a cry
And did so earnestly and not ask yourself why
You didn't have to so it but you did it anyway
Then don't just sit there believe what I say

There are birth mothers that would not treat them like you do
So fear not eve if you are not biological you are a mother too
If you are a woman that is all it takes
For what you go through alone you should be the president of the
United States

You should rule the world, the universe too
For there would not even be a people if there was not you

So every time you see a woman young or old black or white give Her
respect with all your might

She may not be your mother grand if that
But believe me a woman helped you get where you are

Please don't think a man isn't important too but believe me a man
would never survive what a woman has to go through

It is not the man I am putting down it is just an attitude
I'd like to turn around

All women are special, yes you are too for she is the mother of a people
that has created me and yes created you

THE GROOM TO HIS TO BRIDE TO BE

This is the beginning of the rest of my life
The day I become your husband and you my wife

As I vow my love to you, know that it is true
For I begin my new life, I begin it with you

I shall throw in the bachelor towel with pride
As I take your hand and make you my bride

There will no longer be just me and just you
We will be as one and not as two

I cannot promise that every day will be sunshine without the rain
Nor can I promise there will never be pain

I can only say as I vow my love to you this day
That I will try hard to fulfill all your wants and needs I pray

As we begin our lives together
Let us bond better than the finest leather

As we make our vows before god and man
Let us both take our stand

As we journey through the end of our single world
I will hold you dear as if you were a precious pearl

Let us begin on the right accord with our undying love
Let is also praise and thank god above

Know that today, tomorrow and always my love is true
And that I mean it when I say I do

BRIDE TO HUSBAND TO BE

Today is the first day of the rest of my life
The day you become my husband and I become your wife

As I say my vows know that I mean all that I say
I am a very happy woman on this very special day

I know that every day will not be perfect as I would want it to be
But through our love and understanding we will get through anything
you will see

Today is our beginning and the day your bachelorship will end
Not only will you be my husband you will be my best friend

Just to show my love is true
Five, then even fifty years from now
I will still be devoted only to you

Everything will not have to go my way all the time
I will love you if you do not have one dime

As long as we have the things we need to live
As long as you do not just take but also give

I will be at your side and that is where I will always stand
Not only are you my best friend but you are now my husband

Know that as I say my vows today I will say them from my heart
For today we begin our lives together – may we never part

I promise to love, to honor and obey
I promise to love you today and everyday

THE TRUE FRIEND IN YOU

Making everything count in all you do
All that is good comes from inside of you

Respectfully a true friend, yes indeed
You are always willing to help anyone in need

Making people smile is what you are capable of
Everyone you come in contact with can surely feel loved
Remembering special times; birthdays,
anniversaries and other special days

Caring and sharing in so many loving ways
Everyday brings on a new challenge to do
Something special and something so true

Really a true friend I have found – others have too—
We are all glad that we found the true friend in you!

WHAT A MAN

Masculine specimen of a man
Intelligent being that always can

Charming personality, warm as can be
Harmless and so thoughtful of me

Always willing to lend a hand
Everything I ever wanted in a man
Loving, caring and willing to take a stand
Forever my love will belong to you

I will love you my whole life through
Every time we are together, I hate to leave
Loving you is the best thing I've done I do believe

Do always stay the same and always be true
So in return I can do the same for you

GONE TOO SOON

It seems like only yesterday that I held you as you cried
I made you feel better as the tears from your eyes dried
You were so sweet and curious you wanted to know everything
Boy what a joy in my life you did bring

Who would have thought that you would be gone?
It does not seem fair
If I had known, I would have kissed you one last time
And held you so close so very near

That is life we never know when our name will be called
We can only hope and pray for each other – one and all
I will never see you attend the prom or graduate from high school
Of course I know god is the master, we have to play by the rule

I thought that you would mourn me, not that I would mourn you
This is something no parent want to go through
I am strong and full of faith my child
I know that we will meet again,
And we will only be apart for a while

I will miss you and your loving charm
I will miss the way you felt in an embrace in my arms

Sleep on my sweet little one and take your rest
I love you now and always, but God loved you best

I will hold all that was yours dear,
Especially your favorite little spoon
I will forever be grateful for your time here with us
Even if it seems that you were gone too soon…

TAKE TIME

Take time to smell the flowers that grow in god's beautiful garden
Take time to see and appreciate god's great landscape
As you travel the road you are prodding

Take time to feel and sniff the wonderful air God provides
Take time to thank god for your new or old car hey it's a ride

Take time to appreciate every sunrise that break
Take time to be careful of the many choices
You are blessed to make

Take time to say thank you or to apologize
Take time speak – say how do you do as you pass by

Take time to lend a hand while you are able
Take time to bless a friend or neighbor with goodies
Just for their table

Take time to give advice to the youth,
Hoping to reach at least one or two
Take time to take pride in precious favors
And kindness others have given you

Take time to let someone know they are appreciated
Take time to show that kindness shared is not overrated
Take time today before it is too late
Take time to show love to a friend or love mate

Nothing is wrong with being kind, and it does not cost a dime
Go ahead show some love and do not be ashamed to take time

YOU DESERTED US

You walked out on us, yes you did
You left and did not look back
Or even try to check on your kid

I was raised without a male figure at all
Thus, you did not bother to write or call
I thank God for the special mother I got
For she was there for me, as both parents, when you were not

All you really did was plant a seed
You did not water it or give it the care it would need
Anyone could have done what you did, any man at all
You did not even bother to buy my first ball

What happened to your vows: remember to love, honor and trust
You walked out on me and my mother – you deserted us
No birthday card, no Christmas gifts or toys
Growing up, I envied many other little boys

My mother never said one bad word about you to me
She always said "he will come my son, you will see"
You came back but not to reclaim what you left behind then
You put hope in my mother's heart only to disappoint her
Because you left again

You never sent us a home to help us out
I guess you really never knew what being a husband
Or a father was all about

I am now a man and a good one too
All that is because of my mother, not you

I guess I should thank you for what you did not do
Your absence made me grown up sooner, and more thankful
For what I have because of what I have been through

On top of all that I found out about a brother and sister that are in
Another part of town
Their mothers too never once put you down

I told them about what you put us through
Then they told me you deserted them too
Now you want me to accept you and treat you like a father
Why should I? Why should I even bother?

You bring shame to the word and never treated me like a son
Besides that, you are selfish, you never dared about anyone
You were so wrapped up in your own life
That you never thought enough about me or my mother your wife

So try to make me feel the guilt,
You brough on yourself and deserve
You think you can walk back into my life now,
I cannot believe you had the nerve

It will take time to heal the pain you have cause me and my mother
Maybe one day we may forgive each other
But do not blame me because you are at fault
And taking the full blame is a must

Afterall it was your choice – you deserted us

CAN WE TRY AGAIN?

Our love for each other was so strong
Now I wonder what went wrong

We have known each other for many, many years
I can remember many happy moments, special times we have Shared
those are moments in time
I will always cherish
Knowing that true real love can never perish

I care so much about you and I know you care for me
I can see it in the way you act, what else can it be?
I see it in the way you look at me and give that
Winning grin
That is why I want to know--can we try again?

We never really said good-bye,
I guess we just lost touch
I knew it was not right then and I know it now
Because I miss you so much

Everything I see brings back memories of you
You were the only thing I thought I ever did right,
The only friend I ever felt was true

It matters not what happened, where you are now or
Where you have been

I just need to know, my love, can we try again?
Let's try to rekindle the flame that used to burn
Help me put out the flame inside of me and give me
What I yearn

In your arms again is where I want to be
Come back into my life so I can set the pain free
Every time the phone rings I get excited that maybe
It will be your voice on the other end
I let pride stand in the way and I have tried to pretend

But I cannot go on like this without trying to restore our love
Know as well as I do that we fit together like a glove
I know we had our ups and downs but, in every relationship,
Ups and downs do occur

I realize that it will not be easy as they were
I believe in the old saying "things are better the second
Time around"
I want to give our love another chance,
If you do not think it is worth it then please turn me down,

Why would I not want to pull You in
If you do not think we can make it
But we had such a good thing that
I do not want to give up or quit

Every time I see you I still feel warm inside
For I know I love you and would love to have you back
And will be waiting with arms open wide
Not only were you a true and trustworthy friend

You were someone on which I knew
I could always depend
That is why I know we can still make things work
So, tell me can we try, again?

LOVING YOU

I always dreamed of being in love
And having that love returned
I have waited many many years and many years
I have yearned

Now that I am in love with you,
I sometimes cannot believe it's true
I cannot believe I am in love and that love can be so true

Loving you is like winning the lottery
I am rich in love, and I am very thankful that our love
Is blessed by God above

Loving you is like the sunrise the light to start the day
I am so grateful that you send your love my way
Loving you is like a cool breeze-a breath of fresh air
I am so glad that I love you and that you really care

Loving you is like a rainbow--the road to a pot of gold
I want to spend the rest of my life with you;
We can watch each other grow old

It feels so good to love someone and know they love you too
I have what I have always dreamed of yes,
My dream has come true
For I have always dreamed of being in love and
I am glad I am loving you

RELIEF

Reasoning when there is no use;
striving to retain your youth

Ever so faker to understand and always willing
to lend a hand

Lively as can be-remedilessly trying to let all
Anger and pain free eagerly waiting for your dreams
To come me true-always believing in you

If you had one wish you wish for peace and
Unity in every community

Faithful and trusting in the creator; of course,
Nothing else can be greater than that belief
Besides, how do you spell r-e-l-i-e-f!!!

GENTLE LOVING BEAUTIFUL RAIN

As I sit by the window watching the rain come down
I 'feel a since of relief that is why
'The clouds cry rain as fast" that is the belief
Rain, rain go and wash my troubles away
So I can have peace of mind at I fast one day

Wash away the pain that pounds my heart
Take away the bad memories that tears me apart
Cleanse my spirits and ease my pain
Ob, beautiful, loving gentle rain

Flush away anger, hate and defeat
Ease all pain and shall dance to the rhythm of music beat
Water my roots and watch me grow
I long to bloom like a precious flower maybe
I am the seed that you sow me

The beat inside of me cleanse deeply and setting me free
I love to watch as you bit the windowpane
Ob, beautiful loving gentle rain
Sunshine, sleet color even begins to conspire
I realize that.as I feel you washing away all my despair

Birds dancing around as you fall sliding
That you are a joy for us all
Providing us with water to quench our thirst
Flourishing the plants that belief her earth

Sure, if we need to do
On toe stateside it is a strain
But it is always good to see you
Oh, gentle, loving beautiful rain

So often we take too many things for granted not even realizing
That we are match
Sea to shining sea to the tiny twinkle of a star

We fail to see the beauty in the little things around us and that is
why we often have to see so much through her eyes

Pay close attention to surroundings
You may miss scenting or have gained
Yes and always, always be grateful for toe gentle
Loving beautiful rain.

PROUD BLACK WOMAN

Golden brown skin and thick dark course hair
Nothing else is the same; nothing else can compare
Proud to be what I am; I would not change a thing if
I could asking for a voice and a chance to be understood

Thick course hair, yes indeed
It is all mine too, no it is not weaved
Large beautiful brown eyes; yes that is a fact
No I would never wear green, blue or even light brown contacts

I would like to make you understand I am a proud black woman
I cannot speak for you I can only speak for myself, can't you see?
Proud of what I am and what I can
Be yes a proud black woman that is me

I will walk beside my brother not in front of or behind him
Although the chance of him doing the same is none to very slim
My sisters do not frown on me and think I am stuck up
Because I am not

I am just proud of who I am and thankful for what I've got
I may not be rich or driving a fancy car
But I am surviving and driving my own ride by far

Watch me as I go up the latter of success
It may not show in how I look or how I dress

Success is reaching your own goal
You do not know wat my goals are, for you have not been told
Do not think I am conceited for I am just convinced standing high
Looking for my black prince

May he come without a white horse, he can come as he please as Long
as he can fulfill all my needs
I do not ask for much, for pleasing me is an easy task
Seek and you will find or to find out just ask

To my sisters all over the world
You are special in your own way and should be treated like a
Precious pearl give respect and expect it too
Treat others as you would have them treat you

Stand up for what you believe in and ask, do not just command
Be proud of who you are, I am proud of myself
I am a proud black woman

YOU STOOD ME UP

I rushed home took a shower and styled my hair
For I knew pretty soon you, my date, would be there
You are always on time, you are seldom late
I was glad for that because tardiness is something I hate

I purchased a new dress in your favorite shade of blue
I was so excited that I was going out with you
I dressed slowly to make sure everything would look just
Right

Anticipating a good time on this special date tonight
Fully dressed, I looked in the mirror.
To check myself once more
Anytime now I knew you would be knocking at my door
Time was winding down and I started to get upset
For it was time to go and you had not shown up yet

How could you do this to me, I thought I was your buttercup
After waiting another hour or more I knew you stood me up
No I am not Roxanne this was not supposed to happen to me
This is not the evening I dreamed of, not the way it should be

You did not call to explain the facts
You did not call at all to be exact
Days went by no word from you
I never thought this would be something you would do

Then you had the nerve to call me to ask
Why I went out with your friend
Why not ask him, after all the night you stood me up
It was his car you all were riding in

Now you claim I am the one who is wrong for going out with
Another guy
But hey, we both know the reason why
Next time you meet a nice young lady,
You will think twice before standing her up

You will show for each date and arrived early too
For the next time the one who get stood up could be you • • •

ALL GROWN UP

I was making my own decisions about my own fate
Being told what to do was something I really did hate
Playing by my own rules and breaking them too
I was responsible for myself, I did what I wanted to do

I felt that way once, but it did not pay
I am now a young mother and I was not ready, needless to say
I went from pig tails right to pampers and spit up
But that was the price I had to pay, after all I was all grown up

My mother warned me but I did not, heed
Hanging out with my so-called friends,
I though was all I need
I did as I pleased and did what I wanted to do
Take notes or the same thing can happen to you

No going out to the football games or to the school dance
Grew up too fast I did not have time to be a child,
I did not have a chance
I missed so much of my youth by getting off track

The sad thing about it is once it is gone, you cannot get it back
My so-called friends all turned on me
They said my mistakes opened their eyes and helped them to see

Now that I am older, if I had to do it all over
I would make a change
Now I can see that growing up too fast
And not being a child was out of range

I am thankful for my bundle of joy
But sometimes it was hard knowing that instead of holding my
Child I should have been, and wanted to, hold the toy

It was a hard lesson to learn but
I can consider myself fortunate
I am surrounded by caring loved ones who help see
That it was not too late

It was not an easy road to be on
And don't have to be the one you choose
Do not rush to gain so much so soon for in order to gain
You must lose something

Remember, everything grows at a certain pace
Every dog was once a pup
Take your time and be a kid don't rush it
One day you will be all grown up....

THE SECOND TIME AROUND

When we first fell in love,
we were too young to know hat we really had
I was just a little girl and you a young lady
We had a special bond that was very strong
Still, something between us went very wrong

I do not know what it was then,
I just hope it never happens again
You were the first man to kiss me
You made me feel so secure and so free

I could always be myself I never had to pretend
You were not only my lover, you were my best friend
You introduced me to so many new things
You showed me what being a true friend would bring

You were the first to touch me in a loving way
I can still remember how I felt even to this day
You made me realize that I was a woman for sure
You held me tenderly and gently and made me feel so pure

Who would ever guess we would be together again
This time it will last for sure--all the way to the end

If you love something, set it free if it returns it was meant to be
That is exactly what happened to you and me

True love was what we wanted and now it is what we have found
True love indeed, the second time around
Of course, we both have our faults and that is to be expected
We both need our space and our spaces will be respected

In your arms again is where I belong
Hold on to me, never let go and believe in us
In your heart real strong

Safe next to you safe and sound
What could be better than our love the second time around

WHAT DOES AGE HAVE TO DO WITH IT

An older man dating a younger woman it is fine
An older woman dating a younger man to some is almost a crime
What does age have to do with feelings of the heart
Block out age if what you want the youngster is got

Since you came into my life, I have learned plenty of new things
I guess that is what playing the number game will bring
It matters not what they think, because our friendship is true
You are honest with me and I am honest with you

No one will understand what I see in you because of your age
They cannot judge a book by its cover,
They have to read it page by page
You light up my life and make me feel so secure
I am happier than I have ever been to share a love that is so pure

I cannot argue because of course the shoe does fit
But what does age have to do with it
Just because you are younger does not mean I know more,
That is true

It just means that I have occupied space longer than you
Look past our age difference and enjoy each other while we can

No matter what problem I have you always
Listen and always understand

I did not ask for a lifetime commitment
That would not be fair to you
For I have been through so many things that you will
Have to face too

We look and feel good together and that is a fact
Electric shocks go off every time we make contact
Besides, no one can look at us and tell the difference in your favor or
mine

They would have to look really deep to make that find
You make me feel alive, refreshed and complete
Anyone who see us together can see the chemistry
And feel our heat

Let us enjoy our relationship while we can,
Taking it to the limit we cannot quit
Afterall, love has no boundaries
And what does age have to do with it?..

TRIBUTE TO AUNT BEULAH

From nieces and nephews
Auntie you were a pillar of strength and
We all knew that
You were the backbone of our family as a
Matter of fact
Always saying what you meant and meaning
What you did say
No one will ever take your place today
Or any day
A smile on your face and always a question
Or two
Like now who are you? Or which one are you?
We know you are not really gone you are
Just away
We will meet again someplace, someday
As long as we remember you, you will not
Really be gone
Fond memories of you will ensure that you
Forever live on
Someone will have to step up and be the strong hold
For all of us
It is not just a request it is definitely a
Must

If you could say something I believe you would say: "my
Dear ones love one another, stay together and do not
Weep for me
I am in a better place - I will lay down and take my rest
For my soul is free"
So sleep on dear auntie and take your rest, we all
Loved you but god loved you best.

MY VALENTINE

You have changed my life in such a short while
You healed my pains and made my heart smile
May you find in me, what I have found in you
May our friendship grow stronger each day and
Stay true
May I make your gloomy days bright without sun
Rays
May I make you feel special today and all days
Knowing that everything may not always as we
Would like, but will always turn out fine
May you forever share our special bond and always
Be my valentine

A SECOND CHANCE FOR LIFE

E was down and out, so afraid and so alone
Where had all the joy in my life gone
Everything I touched seem to fall apart
Everyone I came in contact with seemed to break my heart

My family turned their back on me and I did not have one friend
I wanted and needed so many things
But did not have a time to spend so filled with
Deceit and despair
I gave up the fight, did not want to live anymore, I did not care

I planned to just take my life but did not have enough courage
I even failed at death, so I became discouraged
When all else failed, I started drinking to ease my pain
Only to realize when I became sober, that I had all my problems
Again

One night I had a dream about a man that said
"Everything would Be alright"
I could not see his face but I felt a change in my life that night

He told me that he would never leave me and that
I would never be alone

He appeared so quickly, gave me those encouraging
Words and then he was gone

I opened my eyes and I saw a bright light
I began to wonder if I really had a dream treat night
I got up early the next morning to start my day
I felt really different somehow and, in some way,

I knew that things was going to be different from then on
All my doubts and worries were all gone
As each day passed, I began to see a little clearer
And feel sharp as a knife

For I now knew and will always know that
I was given a second Chance at life

STEP OUT ON FAITH

When you believe in your heart that something is true
No one can make you change your mind, it is up to you
Believe in your heart that you can do anything with God as
Your guide

Let god take control and come inside
Your troubles will be over, all problems solved
Your prayers will be answered, all worries dissolved
Miracles happen all over the place
There is a miracle waiting for you, rust step out on faith

Ask and ye all receive, seek and ye shall find
That is a promise god made to all mankind
Salvation is free and so is god's grace
So what are you waiting for, step out on faith

Claim what you want in his name
Then go tell someone you know to do the same
It will work for you and other too
Just hold on to your faith it is up to you

When nothing is going right and everyone else
Seem to turn their back

God will still be there and that is a fact
He will never disappear without a trace
Try him you will see, step out on faith

When all doors seem to close on you and there seem to be no
Way out
God will take over and fight your battle, no doubt
If you want something and willing to go get it
No matter what try to stand in your way--do not quit
No one can do it, you have to do it yourself
Go to the heavenly grocery store and take faith
Of the shelf

It will never fail if you believe in god's grace
So what are you waiting for step out on faith!

WHOSE AT FAULT, WHOSE TO BLAME

When all your dreams seem out of touch
And all your hard work do not seem to add up to much

Do not give up or get discouraged
For god will step in and cure all your worries
Cast all your burdens upon our savior is his order
He will take care of everything and fight the battle for you

Put God in total control of your life in full
Then watch all the strings in your life come together as god pull
It matters not where you are or where you have been
Trust in the master he is your friend

Never to leave you in your time of need
A true friend in Christ, a friend indeed
So forget all the excuses, for they are all lame
Who's at fault, who's to blame

Look up for help is on the way
Just trust in the lord and always pray
He will hear your cry day or night
You cannot lose the battle for god is in the fight

Change is something that we are all capable of
I tis possible through god's grace and love
No matter what you have done or been through
There is always someone who has been there too

Repent and give your life to Christ today
On his word depend and on the right path you will stay
We have all come short of the glory of God,
You and me Christ died on the cross for our sins,

He set us free
The devil is busy and always trying to get in
Do not let him take control,
he is not your friend no matter what you are going through
God can prevail

He will never leave you, with Christ you cannot fail
It does not matter what we get here on this side
For there is a reward for you in the arms of
Christ that are opened wide

You have a choice, it is up to you
Choose Christ now and he will see you through
Do not take my word for it, try God on your own
It may seem that you are by yourself but you will never
Again be alone

He will build you up where you are torn down,
Lift you up when you fall
He will do the same for you that he has for me,
He will help us all

Do not gain the world and lose your soul
For it would be a shame
I ask you who's at fault, who's to blame.

www.ingramcontent.com/pod-product-compliance
Lightning Source LLC
Chambersburg PA
CBHW020321130626
46549CB00003B/962